AROUN
CANNOCK
IN OLD PHOTOGRAPHS

THE CENTRE OF CANNOCK at the turn of the century.

AROUND
CANNOCK
IN OLD PHOTOGRAPHS

COLLECTED BY

MARY E. MILLS AND SHERRY BELCHER

ALAN SUTTON
1990

Alan Sutton Publishing
Gloucester

First published 1989
Reprinted 1990

British Library Cataloguing in Publication Data

Around Cannock in old photographs.
1. Staffordshire. Cannock, history
I. Mills, Mary II. Belcher, Sherry
942.4'67

ISBN 0-86299-689-9

Typesetting and origination by
Alan Sutton Publishing.
Printed in Great Britain by
Dotesios Printers Limited.

CONTENTS

The original premises of the *Cannock Advertiser*, founded by Alfred Withington. The first edition of the paper appeared on Saturday, 15 June 1878. It was a 'free' newspaper for the first year of its life.

INTRODUCTION

The area covered by this volume, while focused on Cannock, encompasses much of the central part of the Cannock Chase coalfield, formerly part of the ancient forest of Cank. Thus it covers a mixture of urban centres, mining settlements and also the still wild heathland of the present Cannock Chase.

The town of Cannock is the largest and one of the oldest settlements of this region. Records date back to the Domesday book and later it became an important market centre serving a large region. During the seventeenth and eighteenth centuries several wealthy families were attracted to Cannock because of its healthy location and spa water. However, the district was very sparsely populated until the mid-nineteenth century and Cannock remained relatively small. In 1851 White's Directory of Staffordshire was still able to describe Cannock as '. . .a large and well built village with about 1,100 inhabitants.' After this date the population of Cannock grew rapidly due to the development of coal-mining in the area and the town expanded both to house miners and provide a range of shops and services for the whole region.

Another place that grew rapidly at this time was Hednesford. Originally a small hamlet based on the Cross Keys Coaching Inn on the route from London to the North, it also served as a centre for the trainers who exercised their horses on the nearby Hednesford Hills. In 1851 it was still a very small place with a population of only 308. The whole character of the village was transformed in the 1860s and '70s by a massive influx of miners and it became a small town serving the mining communities which were springing up all over the district.

These communities varied a lot in size and character. Some, like Hednesford, had already existed as villages before mining began on a large scale, and, although they grew larger at this time, continued to be places with their own individual identities. Cheslyn Hay first began as a squatter settlement and its early population was reputed to have included a criminal element with at least one notorious highwayman! This changed during the nineteenth century when the arrival of Methodism in the village encouraged a more respectable type of citizen to settle. Great Wyrley, on the other hand, was mainly a collection of farming settlements although mining on a small scale was established from the eighteenth century. Norton Canes was always a scattered village lying astride the ancient Watling Street. Of all the settlements on the coalfield, Norton has suffered most from problems of subsidence. The people of Burntwood and Hammerwich were mainly farmers and nailers. Both places grew in population due to mining but did not develop into large mining settlements themselves.

By contrast, some mining communities grew from nothing on former common or heathland only recently enclosed. They were sited close to the older settlements but even closer to the newly sunk pits. Some of these grew rapidly to form separate communities in their own right. Chasetown and nearby Chase Terrace were established originally to house workers for the Hammerwich pits owned by the Marquis of Anglesey. They grew in the 1860s under the influence of the Cannock Chase Colliery Company who took over and expanded the pits and soon became separate parishes rather than part of Burntwood and Hammerwich. The colliery company, under its first two managers, J.R. McClean and Arthur Sopwith, played a direct part in the development of Chasetown into a thriving community with a wide range of services and facilities.

Rawnsley, on the other hand, in many ways appears to fit the stereotype of the typical mining village. It was dominated by Cannock and Rugeley Colliery Company and consisted of rows of terraced houses with few amenities.

Heath Hayes presented a further contrast. There was no one all-important colliery company but a choice of pits to work in. A remarkably large percentage of the original houses were built and owned by miners and the village seemed to attract enterprising people.

Other communities that were established in the region depended more on the town of Cannock and did not develop as separate centres to the same extent. Chadsmoor, Bridgtown and Wedges Mills fall into this category.

Before the rapid development of mining this area was dominated by large landed families such as the Pagets, later Marquis of Anglesey, the Littletons (Lord Hatherton) and the Husseys. While some of the land was farmed, much remained as uncultivated commons and heaths. The few industries that existed, mainly nailing, iron working and brick and tile making, were largely small scale and scattered. There had been coal-mining since the Middle Ages but only in very small pits in places where the coal lay near the surface. Apart from the Edge Tool works of William Gilpin at Churchbridge there was no sizeable industry.

After 1860 a new group of industrialists and entrepreneurs such as Harrison, MacClean and Hanbury emerged to replace the older landed families. It was they who developed the mining companies and influenced the new communities. Only existing industries, which were largely related to mining, expanded at this time and virtually no new industry was established. The area's transport system grew considerably with a network of both railways and canals being developed.

Coal production increased rapidly with the entire Chase coalfield producing seven million tons by 1914. A feature of this coalfield in the days before nationalization was the concentration of several large colliery companies who, between them, controlled the industry; Cannock Chase, Cannock and Rugeley, Cannock and Leacroft, West Cannock, East Cannock, Coppice, Great Wyrley and Littleton. The area had a reputation for up-to-date and relatively safe pits. Cannock Chase coal was renowned as the finest quality house coal and was sold in many parts of the country.

By nationalization in 1947 there were 22 collieries operating 33 shafts and one drift mine in the whole Chase coalfield. However, the 1950s and '60s saw a rapid decline in the number of working pits. Today only two pits remain on the entire coalfield; Littleton and Lea Hall. With the closure of the majority of the collieries the character of the area has undergone a further change and today we see the growth of service industries, large shopping complexes and modern housing estates.

The physical evidence of coal-mining in the shape of spoil heaps, chimneys and pit gear, once such a feature of the locality, have now all but disappeared and a new landscape is emerging. One of the values of this collection of photographs lies in the recording of these once familiar scenes. In addition, the period covered, the 1860s to the 1960s, closely coincides with the growth and decline of coal-mining in the area.

As well as recording aspects of the coal industry, the photographs provide a picture of the lives of the people of the area, both at work and at leisure, in times of celebration and distress. They will evoke memories of a fast disappearing way of life for older residents and provide an insight into the area's history for newer arrivals.

Many of these photographs are from the extensive collection held at Cannock library which have been donated both by individuals and institutions, notably the former *Cannock Advertiser*. Other sources include Burntwood library and private collections belonging to local people. This is the first time a collection of photographs covering this area has been brought together for publication.

SECTION ONE

Around the Chase

FIVE WAYS JUNCTION, Heath Hayes. With the exception of the traffic island this view is recognizably the same today.

CANNOCK in 1869. Probably the earliest surviving photograph of the centre of Cannock. The Crown Hotel is on the right. The former Council House is just visible behind the old lime trees bordering the bowling green. The house which later became the offices of the *Cannock Advertiser* stands on the far left.

THATCHED COTTAGE AT THE TOP OF HIGH GREEN, at the junction of what is now Park Road (formerly Simms Lane) and Old Penkridge Road.

THE MANOR HOUSE, CANNOCK. Parts of the building dated back to the seventeenth century. It was sold for £4,450 in 1936 and was demolished within a month of the sale. The Danilo cinema, shops, a car park and Manor Avenue were built on its site.

ST LUKE'S, THE PARISH CHURCH OF CANNOCK taken in around 1895 before the graveyard was levelled.

THE CROWN HOTEL. A very well-known landmark of the old market town of Cannock. It was demolished in 1961. Wright's butcher's shop is to the right.

LOOKING TOWARDS HIGH GREEN, this view can be dated to around 1912.

LINFORD'S SHOP, CANNOCK. The firm of Charles Linford was founded in 1877. The original premises, featured here, are little changed and still in use today. The shop is one of the oldest surviving buildings in the town.

ONE OF THE CONDUIT PUMPS, photographed in 1956, shortly before its removal. Dr William Byrche of Leacroft Hall gave the use of his spring at Rumer Hill to provide the people of Cannock with a proper water supply. Supported by public subscription and endowments the conduit provided water for over two hundred years.

HEDNESFORD ROAD, CANNOCK. Mr and Mrs Tooth in the garden of their farmhouse at the corner or Hednesford Road and Hednesford Street in the early years of the century.

THE OLD SMITHY at the top of Wolverhampton Road. It was kept by blacksmith, George Turner, for many years. His son ran a second smithy in Walsall Road.

THE RAILWAY HOTEL, known locally as The Clocks it stood at the entrance to Cannock railway station.

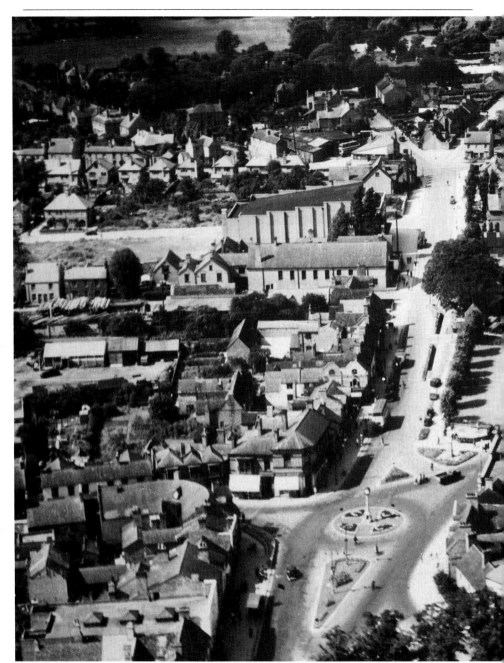

AN AERIAL VIEW OF CANNOCK taken in 1948. Many of the landmarks have now disappeared including; the Market Hall, the Forum Theatre (formerly the Hippodrome), the Co-op, the Danilo. In addition to this much of the farmland in the background has been built on.

CANNOCK TOWN CENTRE around 1960, when buses ran from the side of the bowling green and nobody had thought of pedestrianized shopping areas.

CENTRAL CORNER, BLACKFORDS before 1914. The Central Boot Store later became Vaughan's greengrocers. Seager's butcher's shop stands on the right of the photograph.

MINERS' HOUSES. Nos. 42–47 Cecil Street, Chadsmoor taken in the 1930s and giving an impression of conditions in the time of the depression.

POSTCARD VIEWS OF HEDNESFORD. Looking at these views it is difficult to believe that Hednesford was a thriving mining town with all that that implies. Alfred Williams in 1892 wrote that 'The town always has a busy look about it and contains many well built and attractive looking shops. . . . Some of the streets are very hilly, but the country around is in parts exceedingly pretty, and some very fine views are to be obtained from the neighbouring hills.'

Market St., Hednesford.

TWO VIEWS OF MARKET STREET, HEDNESFORD. The scene above, dating from the turn of the century, suggests a recent spell of bad weather while the view below shows the street in a better light, spruced up for a celebration believed to be the 1911 coronation of George V.

NOS. 48–53 BLEWITT STREET, Hednesford, taken in February 1933. This row of terraces typifies housing erected in the later nineteenth century for the rapidly expanding population. Enoch Blewitt, a famous local character, owned the houses and kept a beer house. He was one of the many landlords who invested in such rows. Note the nice range of advertising enamels.

STAFFORD LAND, HEDNESFORD in the 1920s, long since transformed by modern housing.

OUR LADY OF LOURDES, Hednesford. Opened and dedicated by Dr Williams, Archbishop of Birmingham, on 6 June 1934. This photograph was taken in 1956 and the scene is little changed today.

THE WEST CANNOCK PIT MOUND, May 1945. This view was taken from between houses on the Belt Road. Known locally as the 'fiery heap' it provoked widespread complaints from nearby residents. Housewives battled in vain to keep their washing clean. The conical shape of the mound is very different from the earlier flat-topped spoil heaps. Both were once typical features of the landscape.

THE CROSS KEYS, 'Old Edgeford' (Hednesford). The village centred around the Cross Keys, a former coaching inn built in 1746. The Cross Keys stood on the ancient Blake Street, originally a salt way, which later formed part of an important coaching route from London to the North. This was the main road across the Chase until 1781.

LITTLEWORTH HILL, Hednesford. Evidence of one of the problems caused by extensive mining — houses badly affected by subsidence.

THE RAWNPIKE OAK, NEAR HAZEL SLADE, from which the village of Rawnsley got its name. Believed to have been over 800 years old it was struck by lightning and finally burnt by vandals in the 1930s.

LICHFIELD ROAD, HEATH HAYES. An early view, taken between Five Ways island and Gorsemoor Road.

THE A5 IN MUCH QUIETER TIMES. The *A5* or Watling Street was originally a Roman Road. It was later a drovers' road along which cattle were brought from as far away as Ireland to be fattened for the London market. The name Pinfold is believed to derive from a place where cattle were traditionally penned overnight.

THE FLEUR DE LYS, NORTON CANES. This inn was one of the stops on the drovers' route. The original building dated back to at least the sixteenth century. A notorious court case of the 1580s concerned 'licentious behaviour' at the inn. The building in the photograph was badly affected by subsidence, abandoned for many years and finally burned down in the 1940s. A modern building of the same name now stands in its place.

HALL LANE, Norton Canes was named after Norton Hall demolished earlier this century.

PRINCESS STREET, CHASE TERRACE viewed from the Cannock Road. The cottage on the right still stands today as do several other houses in the picture. Many mining families lived there, especially before 1914.

NORTON POOL, now known as Chasewater, was enlarged by the Birmingham Canal Navigation as a feeder reservoir for the canal system. In those days, as now, a leisure resource for the local population.

CHURCH STREET, CHASETOWN. The chimney of the No. 2 pit of the Cannock Chase Colliery Company can be seen at the end of the street. The cottages in the foreground were originally provided by the Marquis of Anglesey to house colliers working at his Hammerwich pit in the early 1850s. Built at a cost of £40 each they were rented at 2s. a week. They were taken over by the founders of the colliery company in 1857. The rest of Chasetown grew up around these houses.

THE JUNCTION AT THE CENTRE OF CHASETOWN features the clock demolished by a lorry about twenty years ago. The building on the left was the Wesleyan Chapel built in 1884. Note the old petrol pump outside the present bicycle shop.

ST ANNE'S CHURCH, Chasetown. It opened in 1865 and was built at the expense of J.R. McClean, one of the founders of the Cannock Chase Colliery Company. He directed that all 700 seats should be rent free in order to encourage local people to attend. The church is noted for being one of the first to be lit by electricity in 1883. The supply was run under the road from the No. 2 pit along old winding cable.

THE SWAN INN, Burntwood in the 1920s. A noted local landmark then, as now.

HAMMERWICH POST OFFICE in the early years of the century. The original post box was set into the wall of the old school house. Letters came via Lichfield.

GREAT WYRLEY POST OFFICE. In 1900 the sub-postmaster was William Henry Brookes. Letters came via Walsall. They arrived in the village at 7.15 a.m. and were dispatched at 7.15 p.m. Mr Brookes was also a grocer and draper.

NOS. 54–65 WOLVERHAMPTON ROAD, WEDGES MILLS. The houses are believed to have been built by William Gilpin for company workers. Situated between the old canal bridge and the brook bridge they were some of the last 'back to back' housing to be demolished in the district. The houses were pulled down in the 1950s when the road was widened.

LONGFORD CROSSROADS on the A5. The grounds of Longford House, now a restaurant, are in the background.

LONGFORD ISLAND in the 1930s. The road has been widened and a new garage has replaced the earlier buildings. A large traffic island dominates the scene today.

THE HATHERTON EXTENSION CANAL AT CHURCHBRIDGE in 1926. The White Lion Hotel stands near the flight of locks which led up to the Hednesford basin. Locks, canal and hotel have all now disappeared.

WALKMILL LANE, BRIDGTOWN. This tranquil, rural scene shows it as it was. The site is now occupied by industrial units and retail outlets.

WILLIAM GILPIN'S EDGE TOOL WORKS, CHURCHBRIDGE. The firm was founded in 1763, moved to Wedges Mills in 1790 and by 1850 was located at Churchbridge. By this time the firm had a world-wide reputation.

SHOAL HILL COMMON, CANNOCK. The fencing was known as 'the Monkey Rails'. Local youths would congregate there on Sunday as local people took a stroll after church and chapel services.

A HERD OF FALLOW DEER ON CANNOCK CHASE. A reminder of the fact that the Chase was once part of the Royal hunting grounds of the ancient Cank forest.

CNK.152.   GERMAN MILITARY CEMETERY, CANNOCK.

THE GERMAN MILITARY CEMETERY. By far the most important landmark on Cannock Chase today must be the military cemeteries. The original cemetery was for commonwealth soldiers who died in the First World War, many of them Anzacs. The German military cemetery was developed in the 1960s and 1970s to create a fitting resting place for Germans who died in Britain during the Second World War.

THE POST OFFICE TOWER AT PYE GREEN. Erected in 1964; many local children were convinced that it was a rocket launching site.

SECTION TWO

Local People

MINERS' WIVES, CHASETOWN. This photograph, taken from a postcard dated 1912, bore the following message: 'Dear Amy, This is a strike scene at the back of Donaldsons. They are waiting for relief tickets. The Marquis of Anglesey sent the money. I am glad to tell you the strike is over here . . .'

A BACKYARD SCENE from Landywood, Great Wyrley.

HEDNESFORD, No. 32 Anglesey Street. Unfortunately the family concerned is not named. This is one of several photographs of the same address held at Cannock Library.

THE PARK, CROSS STREET, CHESLYN HAY. This was the residence of the Hawkins family, important local industrialists.

THE SELLMAN FAMILY at the rear of their house in Cannock. The Sellmans have been undertakers for over a hundred years in the Cannock area.

THE HEMMINGSLEY FAMILY from Cheslyn Hay in 1913. Mr Hemmingsley owned the horse that pulled the engine for the Cheslyn Hay Fire Brigade.

DIGNITARIES PICTURED OUTSIDE THE COUNCIL OFFICES, Church Street, Cannock around 1917. The Council offices were built in 1880 at a cost of £5,000. Those present include E.A. Orton, Clerk to the Justices (rear, fourth left), C.A. Loxon (with hand on boy's shoulder), Mr Evans (back, first right), Sgt. Owen (second row, first left), Sgt. Murray (front, second left).

A POSTILLION pictured outside the Cross Keys, Hednesford in the nineteenth century. In 1860 the Cross Keys was kept by John Wilkins, also a local farmer. For many years racehorses were stabled at the inn and trained locally.

A LOCAL TRADESMAN, Cannock. Believed to be R. White, founder of R. White's Lemonade and taken at the rear of the Black Horse Inn when it was kept by Sellmans. Note the pigeon baskets behind Mr White.

J.R. MCCLEAN, director of the Cannock Chase Colliery Company and founder of St Anne's Church, Chasetown. This bust is located in the church.

ARTHUR SOPWITH, manager of the company from the death of McClean in 1873. An energetic and enterprising man who took a leading role in local affairs. He was also a noted mining engineer.

CHASETOWN CHURCHYARD BRIGADE. An early example of an environmental task force pictured in the churchyard opposite St Anne's Church. Second from the right is the vicar, Revd George Drury, vicar of Chasetown from 1905 to 1919.

Left: SAMSON BLEWITT STANDING BEHIND THE DOG. Samson was in his seventies when this picture was taken, although he looks younger. He was an enterprising local farmer, landlord and haulage contractor. He made a habit of paying his employees in his beerhouse, The Hatherton Arms in Blewitt Street each week. The newly built pub at Pye Green is named after him. Right: WESSON BELCHER outside his home in Wedges Mills. He was, for many years, an 'auger striker' at the edge tool forge in the village.

DR JOHN KERR BUTTER. A well-known local character who lived on the site of the present police station in Cannock. He was noted for the menagerie he kept. Many different stories exist about how he acquired the animals, whose frequent escapes caused much consternation. Eric Roberts recalls that, in his work as a GP, Dr Butter used iodine as a universal cure-all. The doctor is seen here acting as a special constable.

CANNOCK CO-OPERATIVE WOMEN'S GUILD AMBULANCE pictured in 1911.

THE ANTEDILUVIAN ORDER OF BUFFALOES photographed in Bridgtown School yard in 1930. Friendly Societies played a very important role in all the local communities. Cannock is noted for having one of the earliest friendly societies dating back to the 1780s. Often connected with churches, chapels, or pubs, friendly societies catered for all, including women. They played an important social function as well as providing a form of social security.

REGULARS AT THE YEW TREE INN, Mill Street, Cannock pose for a formal photograph in the 1920s, complete with clay pipes. Safeways supermarket now stands on this site.

THE RAILWAY TAVERN at Norton Canes.

CHASETOWN HORTICULTURAL SOCIETY in Edwardian times. Such societies were a noted feature of the area, especially amongst the mining population. The man with the beard in the centre of the middle row is Elijah Wills. He was headmaster of Chasetown school from 1863 and lived in the town until his death in 1925.

HEDNESFORD TERRITORIAL ARMY BAND photographed in 1910. The unit was commanded by Colonel Williamson, a director of the Cannock and Rugeley Colliery Company.

MISS ANNIE BLAKEMORE, retiring after 43 years as matron of the Hednesford Accident Home, seen here greeting her successor, Miss Dulcie Buckley. She retired in October 1950.

MISS JENNIE LEE. MP for Cannock for many years, seen here with her husband Aneurin Bevan. Seated between them is Miss Ivy Doreen Terry of Norton Canes who they have chosen as beauty queen at the Labour Party anniversary rally in Cannock park, July 1946.

SECTION THREE

Growing Up

THE TOP SCHOOL, CHESLYN HAY. The pupils are winding wool during the First World War, around 1916. The teacher on the far left is Mrs Pearkes. Most schools devoted time to knitting 'comforters' to be sent out to the soldiers at the front.

Top, right. THE MAY QUEEN, John Wood's school, Cannock. A very early photograph taken in the nineteenth century before the time that Mrs Barker was headmistress. John Wood of Paternoster Row, London endowed the school in 1680 for the instruction of the children of Cannock in reading.

Bottom right. A CLASS FROM CHADSMOOR BOYS' SCHOOL in 1918. The headmaster at the time, pictured here, was Mr G. Powis. Even in a mining village such as Chadsmoor there was clearly a wide difference in income.

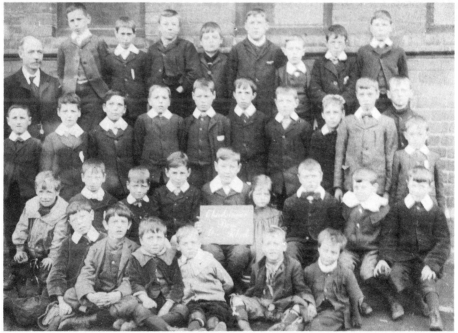

THE HIGHER STANDARD SCHOOL, Chadsmoor pictured on 9 January 1909, soon after its completion. It was described in the *Cannock Advertiser* as '. . . not a pretentious structure. No money has been wasted in unnecessary ornamentation or extravagant decoration.' It cost £4,000 to build and was designed to accommodate 400 children. The first headmaster was Mr Higson and he had eight assistant teachers. More able children from all over the area who had attained Standards 6 or 7 were given places at the school. Former pupils recall science classes in the 1930s presided over by 'Bog Eye' who struck terror in the hearts of all his pupils.

YOUNG PUPILS pictured in the schoolyard of Huntington Church School in Victorian times.

STAFF OF THE ORIGINAL SCHOOL AT CHASETOWN provided by the colliery company, pictured shortly before the First World War. Seated in the middle is Elijah Wills, headmaster, third from left is Weston Cooper, next to him is George Dennis who later became headmaster of Chase Terrace secondary boys' school. Standing second from the right is Mrs Thompson (née Cooke) who taught at the school between 1904 and 1923.

A GARDENING CLASS AT CHADSMOOR MIXED JUNIORS on the Cannock Road, Chadsmoor in 1935. The Methodist church, which still stands today, can be seen in the background.

Bottom, right. INSIDE A CLASSROOM AT CHASETOWN PRIMARY SCHOOL, Church Street in 1930/31, when the children were seven or eight years old. The names are: Standing, left to right: Gordon Dunn, Ted Thompson, Lucy Smith, Albert Baggot, ? Baggely, Don Cook, Fred Downs, -?-, -?-, Tony Dudley, ? Herberts, -?-. Back row, seated: -?-, Muriel Davis, Ida Wolfe, -?-, Derek Taylor, -?-. Next row: Lily Thompson, Harold Turner, Ben Steven, Mary Green, Fred Ruston, Harry Holmes, May Wright. Next row: -?-, Wilf Jackson, Fred Beacham, Doreen Wright, Joan Mountford, Fred Pickering, Walter Hassall. Front row: ? Herberts, Lucy Farr, Horace Nash, Harry Smith, Janet Edgerton, Fred Butler.

AN INFANTS' CLASS at Chasetown school in 1920. The boy at the back with his hand to his head is Eric Shelley. The little girls, first and third from the left on the front row are the Murcott twins.

Heath Hayes
Council Schools, Wimblebury

HEATH HAYES COUNCIL SCHOOLS, Wimblebury Road. This school was one of the original schools set up by the 1870 Education Act and was opened around 1876. The Cannock School Board was set up in 1874. The large detached house in the background belonged to Dr O'Brian for many years.

Bottom, right. LANDYWOOD CHOIR, 1935. The junior choir won five first class certificates for singing and country dancing at the County Music Festival. The teachers are, headmaster, Mr P. Bickford and Miss D. Jones. The High School at Great Wyrley, which includes Landywood, still has a very strong tradition of musical success today.

PUPILS OF NORTON CHURCH OF ENGLAND SCHOOL in 1928. This was a National school built in 1860 and had a school house attached. Both have now been demolished.

Landywood
School Choir
1935.

MR DAVID GARDINER, headmaster of Great Wyrley Secondary Modern from 1953 to 1960 seated between deputies Miss Wilson and Mr Bale pictured with senior pupils. Mr Gardiner was headmaster of three schools in turn: Chadsmoor Boys', Great Wyrley and Calving Hill. Although he retired in 1973, he is still remembered with affection and respect by many local people.

AREA SCHOOL SPORTS, Burntwood Stadium. These sports were an annual event from 1947 until 1966/7. They attracted schools from as far away as Walsall Wood and Shelfield.

THE 1ST HEDNESFORD GIRL GUIDES at camp in Penmaenmawr in 1926. The troop was based in St John's Methodist Schoolroom, Station Road, Hednesford.

A GROUP OF SCOUTS from St Luke's, Cannock at camp in August 1946. The occasion was an international scout camp held at Beaudesert involving 1,500 scouts from all over Europe. The boy with the huge grin in Keith Hopwood of Ebenezer Street, Hednesford.

SECTION FOUR

At Work

ROAD REPAIRS in Union Street, Bridgtown.

LEWIS' TILERIES. An important local industry was brick and tile manufacturing. This photograph, taken in the 1920s or '30s, is of their Rosemary and Walkmill Works and shows the directors and management.

HAWKINS TILERIES in the 1950s. Another important company in this particular industry is Hawkins, now part of the Tarmac Group. The firm was established in the 1840s and has produced roofing tiles at its Watling Street works, Bridgtown, from the mid-1800s to the present day.

WHITEHOUSE BROS. FOUNDRY at Bridgtown around 1925. Mr Arthur Haynes is pictured at the foundry. In 1975, aged 78, he recalled a working day, lasting from 6 a.m. to 5 p.m. making tools by 'very crude methods.' Also shown are Mr Ernest Ellesmore (second from right) and Mr Richard Wenlock (front right).

GREEN LANE, BRIDGTOWN, during the construction of the mineral line to the Mid Cannock Colliery.

STEAM PLOUGHS at work on Prairie Farm, Broadway, Pye Green, in around 1912. The name of the farm seems apt as there are no hedges in sight.

TRADITIONAL HAYMAKING. This scene shows hay being gathered on fields owned by Cannock Chase Colliery Company. The hay was used to feed the pit ponies and the company employed a manager to run its farm which also provided employment for miners laid off in the slack summer months.

Right: MR HUSSELBEE, with his son John, haymaking at a farm in Dartmouth Road, Cannock. Left: ERIC ROBERTS who later became a noted local councillor, pictured in 1927 working as a delivery boy for the Cannock Co-operative Society.

DELIVERY SERVICE from Clarke's Department Store, Cannock. This photograph leaves questions unanswered. It is not clear what is being delivered, nor whether it was usual to employ a girl to do this work. It may indicate that the photograph was taken during the First World War.

CLARKE'S SHOP FRONT in Market Place, Cannock. Dating from around 1910 this gives a clear picture of the wide range of goods they sold. Kelly's Trade Directory of 1900 lists, 'Clarke, Daniel Wheelwright, ironmonger and house furnisher.' He founded the firm in 1878. The original premises in Mill Street burned down at the turn of the century.

EMPLOYEES OF THE CANNOCK CHASE LAUNDRY, Chadsmoor outside their workplace.

THREE PHOTOGRAPHS of Cannock and District Co-operative Society all taken in 1911. The top one shows the front of their store in Church Street, Cannock.

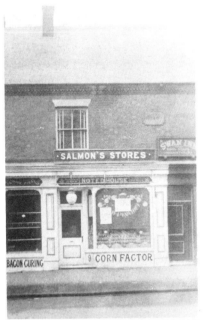

THE BOTTOM LEFT, occupied at this date by Salmon's Stores, was their original premises, opened in 1890. THE THIRD PHOTOGRAPH shows branch No. 5 situated in what is now Cardigan Place, Hednesford.

MRS COOPER'S SHOP, Norton Canes. There was little employment for women in this area but one relatively common occupation was shop-keeping. Mrs Cooper stands outside her shop in Chapel Street. Percy Shaw of Norton Canes recalls that her window display frequently featured nothing but Peak Freans' biscuits.

MRS ELIZABETH LLOYD of Mill Street, Cannock. Her shop sold groceries, tobacco and beer in 1914.

Left: SARAH MARSTON HARRIS at her shop in John Street, Chadsmoor. She and her husband, Captain Daniel Marston Harris, ran the shop for 30 years. He was a war hero, veteran of the Egyptian and South African campaigns and died in 1926. Residents recall that they sold anything and everything. They also kept a parrot in the shop who was noted for reciting rude songs. Right: WIDOW, MARY CLEWLEY, kept a sweet shop next to the old Greyhound public house in High Street, Chasetown. The girl in the photo is her daughter.

HEATH HAYES BAKERY. This business was started by an enterprising local miner, Albert Edward Foster, born in 1866. His wife ran the shop while he baked the bread and worked in mining. He later became a farmer at Chorley. He is pictured with his wife Maud and some of his family, probably in around 1909.

Mining

AN EARLY GROUP of Cannock Chase miners.

NORTON CANES, No. 3 pit, in around 1880. This pit was also called Jerome's as it was owned by the father of Jerome K. Jerome, the well-known author.

TWO PIONEERING UNDERGROUND PHOTOGRAPHS taken by Arthur Sopwith in the Cannock Chase Colliery pits. Underground furnaces, situated at the bottom of shafts formed part of the ventilation system.

AN OVERMAN'S CABIN. The overman supervised work underground.

ENTRANCE TO THE DRIFT MINE near Chasewater which connected No. 1 and No. 2 pits. The men are members of the excavation gang, awaiting the arrival of the first tub of coal.

A BOY LEADING A PIT PONY. One of the first jobs that boys did when they went underground was to lead the pit ponies that pulled the coal tubs.

Underground Workmen 65 To 81 Years Old
Employed by The Cannock Chase Colliery Co Ltd

ELDERLY EMPLOYEES of the Cannock Chase Colliery Company. This company had a reputation for allowing elderly miners to continue working underground for as long as they wished. Their pride in the tradition is shown in this special photograph depicting such workers, all aged between 65 and 81 years. The man with the bowler hat is the overman, William Thompson. Sitting beside him, arms folded, is his brother Charles. The other bowler-hatted gentleman is reputed to have run home to change into his Sunday best when he heard that the photograph was to be taken.

THE CANNOCK AND HUNTINGTON COLLIERY (now the Littleton Colliery) in its early days. The original shaft was sunk in 1877 but serious flooding halted the operation and the colliery was wound up in 1881. The company was re-formed in 1898.

THE COPPICE COLLIERY at Heath Hayes was founded by the Hanbury family in 1892. Most colliery wagons were boldly identified in a bid to prevent a high rate of loss.

THE OLD COPPICE COLLIERY, Lodge Lane, Cheslyn Hay.

THE MID CANNOCK COLLIERY in 1948. Part of this site, at the back of Rumer Hill, is still used as an opencast coal collection point.

THE VALLEY PIT, HEDNESFORD, one of the Cannock and Rugeley collieries. It is now the site of the Valley Heritage Centre and was formerly used as the Mines' Rescue Station for the area.

CANNOCK CHASE COLLIERY COMPANY No. 3 Pit, known as 'The Plant'. The winding house can be seen on the left. This is now the site of British Coal's area workshops and lies off the Lichfield Road in Chase Terrace.

THE DEMOLITION OF THE CANNOCK AND LEACROFT CHIMNEY STACK. Such a sight was a regular feature during the 1950s and '60s marking the end of coal-mining as it had once been.

MEN COMING OFF SHIFT at the West Cannock No. 5. It is believed to be in the 1950s. The austere working conditions, even in a relatively modern pit, are clearly shown.

TWO UNDERGROUND VIEWS showing some mining processes. Above hewers can be seen cutting coal at a longwall coal face.

THIS MAN IS 'RIPPING', the process of making a new roadway or widening an existing one. The photograph was taken at No. 8 pit Heath Hayes in 1962.

THE SAME COLLIERY in 1937 showing men working the brooch seam which produced particularly good house coal. Left to right: W. Bedford, T. Heath, G. Bentley, E. Fitch, Deputy, A. Stanley, N. Hales.

A CONCERT DOWN A MINE! The first ever celebrity concert to be held down a pit, in this area, took place at Harrison's No. 3, Great Wyrley in January, 1943. The tenor, Trevor Jones, had himself been a stallman in a Welsh pit. The other three artists were Mary Lake (soprano), Joan Davis (pianist) and Harold Fairhurst (violin). The violinist, being well over 6 ft tall had difficulty in choosing a spot where he could wield his bow without breaking it against the roof. About 300 miners attended the concert.

THE MINES' RESCUE TEAM from Harrison's No. 3 pit, Great Wyrley. They were first prize winners for three successive years in the annual Cannock Chase Coalowners' Association competition. The members of the 1948 team are: W. Kendrick, (captain), A. Wilson, G. Rounds, W. Fellows, V. Llewelyn, G. Newman, (lieutenant).

ANOTHER PRIZE-WINNING GROUP. This time the Cannock and Leacroft rescue team photographed in 1936, the team comprised: H. Bird (captain), H. Saffhill, W. Wood, E. Owen, C. Mellor and W. Beeston (lieutenant), pictured with colliery officials.

A COLLIERY SURFACE WORKER at the Mid Cannock Colliery, Rumer Hill, Cannock in July 1953.

THE LOCO 'FOGGO' named after a Cannock Chase CC manager. The 'Foggo' may look old-fashioned but it was, in fact, constructed in 1946 using spare parts from the company workshop which would otherwise have been disposed of on nationalization.

THE CENTRAL WORKSHOPS, Norton Canes. Few pictures survive of ancillary services such as workshops which built and serviced mining machinery. All the large companies had their own workshops. Pictured above are the central workshops at Norton Canes some time after nationalization.

THE ACCIDENT HOME at Hednesford, opened in July 1986. Formerly Ford House and built in around 1870. The home began with four beds. It was supported by the Cannock Chase Coalowners' Association, miners and other organisations.

THE LEGACY OF WIDESPREAD MINING. Subsidence at the corner of Belt Road and Pye Green Road in May 1931.

Times of Distress

A MINING DISASTER. These two grim pictures record the tragic events at Brindley Heath on 16 May 1933. A firedamp explosion at West Cannock No. 5 killed six men and left many others badly burned. This picture shows an official with plans of the mine leading out the rescue team.

THE EXPRESSIONS ON THE FACES of the men reveal their feelings as they carry one of their dead colleagues from the pit.

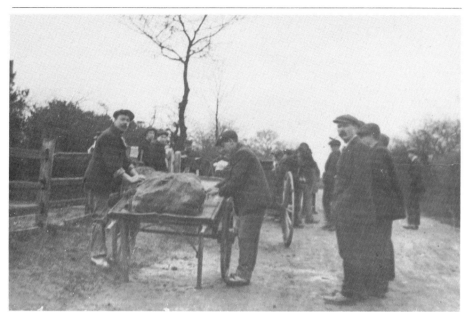

COAL PICKERS DURING A MINERS' STRIKE. This photograph of pit mound pickers at Leacroft, Cannock belonged to Mr B. Withington. He wrote on the back: 'most pickers had to contend with bassinets and go carts and soap boxes to take away the coal but a few "aristocrats" either possess or have hired hand and horse carts, their loads being too big to carry on their backs in bags.' It dates from 1912.

COAL PICKERS ON WEST CANNOCK COLLIERY PIT MOUND during the prolonged strike of 1926. This was a typical sight in times of distress. Men, women and children resorted to searching the waste mounds for coal.

THE MINERS' STRIKE, 1912. These two photographs record events in Cannock between 28 March and 6 April. Following rioting at Littleton Colliery, 500 men from the West Yorkshire regiment were billeted in the town. There was no further trouble and by the end of the week, when the troops had left, the *Cannock Advertiser* was able to report 'No-one will have any but pleasant memories of the stay of the regiment . . .' In fact, it was felt the presence of the troops was 'a welcome diversion in the ordinary quiet life of the town'. The regimental band played on the bowling-green each night and Colonel Cayley, the commanding officer, wrote to thank the people of Cannock for making them so welcome.

A.J. COOKE, a noted miners' leader, addresses a miners' rally at Heath Hayes during the 1926 strike. After this meeting he went on to address another gathering at Pelsall.

GREAT WYRLEY SOUP KITCHEN in 1921. During miners' strikes it was usual to provide soup for the schoolchildren.

LLOYD'S BUTCHER'S AT BLACKFORDS. During the 1926 strike, food for the soup kitchen was cooked at the shop. The food was provided by generous Birmingham traders.

LLOYD'S SOUP KITCHEN CHILDREN. These children received soup and bread one day and cocoa and cake the next.

THE BACKS OF HOUSES IN BRADFORD STREET, HIGHTOWN in 1935. They give a clear impression of the poverty of the times.

A FORBIDDING STUDY and a grim reminder of times past. The Cannock Union Workhouse built in 1872 at the cost of £8,000. It was enlarged in 1886 at a further cost of £800. Kelly's Directory in 1900 describes it as 'A well ventilated building with detached fever wards and now capable of containing 300 inmates.' The master was Frederick Garland Roach and his wife was the matron.

SECTION SEVEN

Celebration

A BEACON AT CASTLE RING. This huge bonfire was built by scouts and guides to celebrate the Silver Jubilee of King George V in 1935. It was lit on 6 May and was followed by a torchlight tattoo and community singing led by the Salvation Army.

A GREAT WYRLEY BONFIRE to be proud of! Built entirely from railway sleepers this bonfire also celebrated the Silver Jubilee.

THE CENTRE OF CANNOCK decorated for the same event.

THE OPENING OF BLACKFORD'S WESLEYAN MISSION in August 1907. The ceremony was performed by Mr J. Williamson. The Reverend William Hunt conducted the opening service. The chapel stood just to the left of the Central Cinema, which now houses business premises.

THE LAYING OF THE FOUNDATION STONE of the Bethel Church at Bridgtown in August 1909.

A SUNDAY SCHOOL DEMONSTRATION, held in 1910 in Market Street, Hednesford. Large demonstrations like this, of 2,000 or more people, were a feature of the area in the first half of the twentieth century. It was an occasion for everyone to turn out on the streets in their best clothes and parade with other members of their chapel.

A SUNDAY SCHOOL TREAT IN CHASETOWN in 1909, showing how the streets were decorated for the occasion. The children joined together in a procession while the adults looked on.

A WEDDING GROUP from Hednesford in Edwardian times.

CROWDS CELEBRATE the coronation of Edward VII. It was the custom, in the days before television, for large crowds to gather in the centre of towns to commemorate national events.

THE BANDSTAND IN CANNOCK. It was erected in 1902 to commemorate the coronation of Edward VII. It is seen here decorated to celebrate the coronation of George V.

A CHASETOWN FOOTBALL TEAM on a triumphal tour of the village, pose outside the Cottage Spring pub in Queen Street.

'COAL HELPED TO WIN THE VICTORY'. An ingenious float, probably part of a procession to celebrate the ending of the First World War.

CANNOCK FLOWER SHOW. Another popular local event was the annual flower show. These photographs were taken in Cannock at the flower shows of 1910 and 1911. Such events attracted huge crowds, over 10,000 people visited the 12th annual show in 1910. They were held on land off Simms Lane and were more than just horticultural shows. Other attractions included brass bands, displays of all kinds and show jumping. One popular feature was the competition for the best turnout of horses and carts. The winners in 1910 were Messrs Evans and Maiden of Dudley.

FESTIVAL OF BRITAIN CELEBRATIONS. Teacher Miss Cross, with children from Great Wyrley Secondary Modern school celebrating the Festival of Britain in 1951. They were dressed as 'Dancers of the British Isles'. The festival was an opportunity for the people to mark the end of a decade of austerity.

Notable Events

THE PROCLAMATION OF THE DEATH OF QUEEN VICTORIA and the accession of Edward VII in 1901, in the Market Place, Cannock.

PROCLAMATION IN HEDNESFORD outside the Anglesey Hotel. J. Hunter, chairman of Cannock Council and managing director of the Cannock and Leacroft colliery reads out the proclamation of the accession of George V.

GENERAL BOOTH, founder of the Salvation Army, visits Cannock. Mr Winton, a member of the Salvation Army, recalled being present on this day and said that General Booth 'looked just like Moses'. The General spoke at the New Hall. He also visited Hednesford in 1885 to lay the foundation stone of the Barracks. A nearby street is named after him.

KING GEORGE VI AND QUEEN ELIZABETH visit Cannock in the 1940s.

WHERE · THE · VICTIM · WAS LAST · SEEN · ALIVE.

THE · SfC · WALL · OVER · WHICH · THE · MUTILATED BODY · WAS · TAKEN · TO · THE · HIDING · PLACE.

NOCK CHASE MURDER.

WHERE · THE BODY · WAS · FOUND.

THE VICTIM. MRS GASKIN.

HEDNESFORD. FEBRUARY. 1919. FUNERAL · OF · THE VICTIM. MAR·2·1919.

THE GASKIN MURDER is still remembered today by local people. Mrs Gaskin was murdered and dismembered by her husband, Henry Thomas Gaskin. He had returned from active service in the war to discover that his wife had been unfaithful and they separated. Mrs Gaskin was killed after receiving a note from her husband and going to meet him in lonely woodland. Despite pleas for clemency Mr Gaskin was hanged.

E SPOT WHERE THE LIVING HORSE WAS
UND GRAZING

WHERE THE ENTRAILS OF THE
DEAD HORSE WERE FOUND.

THE
CATTLE MAIMING OUTRAGES
AT
GREAT WYRLEY.

BROOMHILL FARM. WHERE THE OUTR
WAS COMMITTED.

THE CORNER OF THE FIELD WHERE
HORSE WAS FOUND.

WYRLEY PARISH CHURCH.

'THE WYRLEY GANG' KILLINGS. The village was the scene of a spate of vicious animal maimings and killings between February and August 1903. (Other, isolated incidents, followed later.) George Edalji, a Birmingham solicitor and son of the local vicar of St Mark's was convicted on flimsy circumstantial evidence. He served three years of a seven-year sentence before being released by the Home Secretary. Sir Arthur Conan Doyle became interested in the case and produced evidence which pointed at another local man. The debate still rages as to who was actually guilty.

A PROCESSION through the centre of Cannock. Among notable locals are the Reverend Edalji (front, left) and Mac Wright (pitman) (second row, right).

RULES

AND

REGULATIONS

RESPECTING THE

TRAINING GROUND

TO BE OBSERVED BY THE

TRAINERS, JOCKEYS, HEAD BOYS, & BOYS,

At Hednesford, in the parishes of Cannock & Rugeley.—1866.

RULE 1—Any Trainer intending to have a trial, is to send a written notice to all the other Trainers, and in their absence to the person in charge of the stables, to state he is going to have a trial the following day between the hours of eleven and three o'clock; such notice to be delivered before six o'clock on the Evening preceding the day he intends trying. Should two or more Trainers want the ground on the same day, they must arrange amongst themselves as to the hour they will be on the ground.

2—If any Trainer, Jockey, or Stable Keeper, is convicted of watching a trial, when notice has been given to the Trainers, they shall pay a penalty of Ten Pounds.

3—All Grooms or Boys who are convicted of watching a trial, (notice of it having been given,) shall be discharged by their Employers, and not be again employed by any Trainer or Stable Keeper in Hednesford, under a penalty of Ten Pounds.

4—Should any Boy, Groom, or Servant, who has been convicted of watching a trial, prove that he was ordered to do so by his Master, he shall be acquitted, and the Master shall be fined Ten Pounds.

5—If either Jockey, Trainer, or Stable Keeper, takes any person into his service who has been convicted of watching a trial and discharged from his situation, he shall pay Ten Pounds.

6—Every Horse that is trained upon Hednesford Hills, and others which may come to any Stable at Hednesford, and are exercised on the Training Ground, shall pay ten shillings towards the Training Fund, &c., if only for one day. Every Trainer, Jockey, Groom, or Person is requested to make an honest return of the number trained or exercised by himself, or by his directions. For every Horse in excess of his return, he shall pay One Pound.

7—All strange Grooms who may come to any stable in Hednesford, shall be made acquainted with the Rules and in case they or any of their Boys under them, shall watch any trial, notice of it having been given to the parties, such Jockey or Groom, shall pay Ten Pounds, if they or their Boys under them are convicted. No Groom or Jockey objecting to these Rules, to be taken in by any Trainer, Stable Keeper, &c., in Hednesford. Trainers or Stable Keeper, at whose house strange Grooms may stand with Horses, to be responsible for the penalties being paid on conviction.

8—If any Tradesman or Labourer in Hednesford or in the Neighbourhood, is found lurking or watching a trial, he shall not be employed by any Trainer, Jockey, or Stable Keeper in Hednesford; and if proved that such person is employed, the person dealing with, or employing him or them, shall pay Ten Pounds.

9—If any Trainer, Jockey, or Groom, shall open the preserved ground by removing any Hurdles, Dolls or Gorse, (except for a Trial,) or galloping over the Gorse in any way whatever, they shall pay Five Pounds; and unless the Hurdles, Dolls, Gorse, &c., be replaced within two hours after the trial, he shall pay Two Pounds. Should any Boy remove any Hurdles, Dolls, Gorse, &c., he must be discharged by his employer; and any Trainer, Jockey, or Stable Keeper, employing the said Boy, shall be fined Five Pounds.

RACING ON HEDNESFORD HILLS. Hednesford Hills were long famed for the training of racehorses. A book written in 1892 says about the Cross Keys: 'Here is . . . extensive stabling for blood horses of which about 100 are generally trained in the season and exercised on the excellent turf of Hednesford Hills.'

TOM COULTHWAITE. One of the best known local trainers, he came to the area in 1899 from Manchester. For many years his stables were at Hazel Slade. He produced three Grand National winners; Eremon in 1907, Jenkinstown in 1910 and Grakle, picture below, in 1931. Coulthwaite is also remembered as a generous benefactor to local people, especially the miners of Hazel Slade. He died, aged 88 in 1949.

SIR ALAN COBHAM'S AIR DISPLAY visits Heath Hayes in 1936. Sir Alan Cobham toured Britain and Ireland for 4 years, visiting over 800 towns. His team gave 1,900 performances before 3,000,000 people. He carried 600,000 passengers as part of his policy of 'Flying For All'. By 1936 his display was being run by Mr C.W.A. Scott.

SCOUTS FROM BEAUDESERT SEEK SHELTER in Hednesford following widespread flooding in July 1931. The torrential rain caused widespread damage. The flood made such an impression on people that they can still recall exactly what they were doing on that day.

THE WATLING STREET under five feet of water on 1 July 1958. A lorry is barely visible. Many local places suffered serious flooding that day.

CHURCH ROAD, NORTON CANES, March 1947. This winter lives in many memories as one of the most severe. Norton Canes was cut off for more than six weeks. Local people recall milk and bread being delivered to the square and being collected using upturned kitchen tables as improvised sledges.

COPIES OF THE *CANNOCK ADVERTISER* being delivered by tractor in February 1947.

CONDITIONS IN CHADSMOOR. The extent of the drifts in 1947 can clearly be seen outside Lloyd's corn merchants (formerly a butcher's shop) on the corner of Heath Gap Road.

PRICE STREET, Cannock, during the severe winter of 1963.

'THE SOWER'. This controversial statue was commissioned to stand outside the newly-built Cannock Public library.

CANNOCK CHASE BURNED during the summer of 1976. Hundreds of local volunteers battled alongside the fire brigade to limit the terrible damage wrought by fires following the prolonged drought.

Transport and Services

HEDNESFORD RAILWAY STATION before 1875 when the station bridge was built.

THE MINERAL LINE CROSSING just above the Cross Keys, Hednesford. This railway linked the Cannock Wood Colliery to the Hednesford canal basin at East Cannock.

CANNOCK RAILWAY STATION in Victorian times.

THE PADDY TRAIN. This special train carried miners to and from work at the Cannock Wood colliery, owned by the Cannock and Rugeley Colliery Company.

THE STEAM ENGINE 'The Rawnsley No. 4' built in 1867 by Lilleshall and Co. and pictured here in March 1957. The train is pulling empty box wagons.

COAL LOADING AT THE ANGLESEY WHARF, Chasewater. Hundreds of boats were loaded each week to carry coal to Midland towns.

Canal Side, Hednesford.

THE HATHERTON EXTENSION. This canal lead from Leacroft to the coal wharf at Hednesford. The Hatherton extension was the last working canal to be built, in 1860.

ONE OF A FLEET OF BUSES belonging to the London and North Western Railway Company. This service ran between Brownhills Station and Chase Terrace via Chasetown. The bus is pictured in lower High Street, Chasetown.

A LNWR BUS at Hednesford station. This service ran to Brownhills station via Norton Canes in the 1920s.

MIDLAND RED BUSES in Market place, Cannock, in the 1930s.

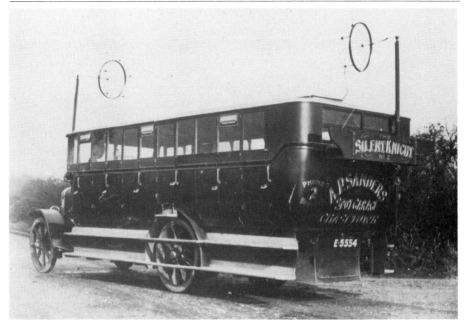

A THORNYCROFT COACH. Part of the fleet operated by A.P. Saunders from the Spot Garage, Chasetown. The equipment on the roof was a very early radio system installed by the proprietor.

THE ORIGINAL SPOT GARAGE at Chasetown in the 1920s. A modern garage of the same name still stands on the site today.

THE POWER STATION AT CHASE TERRACE. It belonged to the Cannock Chase Coal Company and was situated at the No. 5 pit site, Cannock Road, Chase Terrace. The company supplied excess electricity to nearby villages.

THE CANNOCK FIRE BRIGADE in 1927.

SECTION TEN

Wartime and Austerity

PRIVATE J. TOMKINSON. Killed in Action in 1918. He was a member of the South Staffordshire Regiment. Such photographs appeared weekly in the *Cannock Advertiser*, each with their own sad story to tell.

SAPPER THOMAS BROUGH. He worked for 25 years at the East Cannock Colliery and was killed at the age of 46 by a sniper's bullet, on Christmas Day 1917.

THE CHASETOWN DETACHMENT of the Royal Army Medical Corps leaving for Active Service, 26 October 1914.

HUT BUILDERS aboard the 'Tackeroo Express' in 1915. A branch line was hurriedly built from Hednesford station onto the Chase to carry workers building the Army training camps early in the First World War. The trains constantly ran out of steam due to the steep gradients.

THE MILITARY HOSPITAL AT BRINDLEY HEATH. In addition to training camps a Military Hospital was built on the Chase at Brindley Heath near Hednesford. Patients and nurses are seen here during a spell of severe weather.

THE SOLDIERS' CLUB at Hednesford in 1916. Over 20,000 soldiers were stationed in the Chase camps during the First World War. Many local people found employment catering for their needs and voluntary groups also did their best to make their stay more comfortable.

INSIDE HAMMERWICH HOSPITAL during the First World War. This hospital normally catered mainly for miners and both colliery managements and mine workers paid towards its upkeep. This ward is named Cannock Chase Colliery Company Ward. The Matron is pictured with some of her patients.

HEATH HAYES MEMORIAL GATES. The man wearing the patch is G. Jones.

THE UNVEILING OF CANNOCK WAR MEMORIAL in May 1923. A poignant occasion for many people.

THE CANNOCK CHASER SPITFIRE 15 November 1941. Local people raised £6,112 9s. 10d. towards the cost of this Spitfire.

THE CHESLYN HAY HOME GUARD outside the Working Mens' Club in 1945.

A WARTIME NURSERY. This wartime day nursery in Hall Court Lane, Cannock, was established so that mothers engaged in war work could leave their children in good hands. The Matron was Miss K.A. Smith. It was opened in 1943 and set up by the Public Health Committee Chairman, Mr Arthur Hampton. There were two other nurseries in the district at Chadsmoor and Hednesford.

THE WAR EFFORT, Hednesford WVS organize an aluminium collection in July 1940.

LOCAL STREET PARTIES held to celebrate the end of the war in Europe in 1945. Victory party held at the Unicorn Inn, Price Street, Cannock.

NORTON LANE, Great Wyrley, Saturday 12 May 1945. This victory tea catered for 74 children and 60 adults. It was organized by women from Huthill Lane, John's Lane and Norton Lane. Each child received a packet of sweets made and given by Mr and Mrs Bullock. Five shillings was given to 26 residents over the age of 60 and the remainder of the collection was sent to the 21 men and women in the services from the three lanes. The gifts were distributed by Mr and Mrs Handley.

THE MEMORIAL GATES, GREAT WYRLEY. Dedication of the War Memorial plaques at Benton's Lane Recreation Ground, Great Wyrley, attended by members of the Parish Council, British Legion and many local people. They were dedicated by the Revd. T.R. Parker and unveiled by General Sir Oliver Leese on 17 May 1952.

THE WAR MEMORIAL, HEDNESFORD. Built on land given by the Marquis of Anglesey, the War Memorial grounds at Hednesford remain a peaceful haven today.

THE START OF MEALS ON WHEELS. The service began in April 1948, under the supervision of Mrs Wm.C. Speedy. On the first day 36 dinners were given out in Hightown, Littleworth and Cannock Wood, price tenpence. The first meal went to Mr Albert Henry Branson of Queen Street, Hightown. Mrs Branson is here accepting the sweet.

'THEY BROUGHT IT BY THE TON'. Members of the Danilo Chums' Club respond to a salvage appeal in April 1948. The Danilo cinema is the collection point. That day 19 prizes were awarded for effort.

THE GATE of No. 11 School Recruit Training, RAF Hednesford in 1953. Opened in 1938, RAF Hednesford served as a training centre during the Second World War and housed men on National Service until 1956. Some of the huts now form part of the Marquis Drive Visitors' Centre on the Chase, once part of the camp.

MEN OF 6TH FLIGHT ON PARADE.

THE END OF SWEET RATIONING. 'Sweet Sunday' in April 1949 is celebrated in Cannock. Barbara Barr, aged seven, with a bag of barley sugars, the first time in her life she has not bought sweets on ration. She is being served by Mrs L. Cross.

SECTION ELEVEN

Leisure Hours

SANGERS' CIRCUS making spectacular progress down Wolverhampton Road, Cannock. The size of the crowd indicates what a great attraction such an event was for local people. The live lion, chained to the lady on top of the wagon, would certainly not be allowed today.

THE WAKES. One of the major social events all over the area was the annual Wakes. These were organized by various bodies such as churches, public houses, colliery companies and friendly societies and took place in many of the towns and villages. This poster advertises a Wake held at the Roebuck Inn, Stafford Road, Cannock in 1876. Attractions included sideshows, sports and rides.

CHASETOWN WAKES 1922 held on Mrs Meacham's field, site of the present Burntwood Leisure centre. This Wake started in 1865 to celebrate the opening of St Anne's Church and was held in a field opposite the church until 1919. It was organized by the management of Cannock Chase Colliery Company and was held on weekdays. The miners were allowed a half day off to attend.

GYMNASTS FROM CHASETOWN INSTITUTE performing at the Wakes in 1910. The Institute was built in 1888 at a cost of £700 and known to locals as the 'Entertainment Hall'. It contained a large meeting room, reading room, billiard room and smoke room. A bowling green and tennis court were situated close by.

A GROUP POSING IN FANCY DRESS during Bridgtown Carnival around 1935.

THE ELECTRIC PALACE, HEDNESFORD. It was, in its time, both a cinema and skating rink. Before the days of television such local attractions were far more common than today. Most, like the Electric Palace, have now disappeared.

THE DANILO CIMEMA, opened in 1939. It was one of several cinemas in Cannock at that time. The building was demolished and replaced by a supermarket in the 1960s. The name lives on in nearby Danilo Street.

BRIDGTOWN FOOTBALL CLUB 1906. There were many football clubs throughout the region based on public houses, colliery companies, friendly societies and churches. This team obviously had a successful year in 1906.

HARRISONS COLLIERY FC at the end of the 1936/7 season. They won the Bloxwich League Challenge Cup, Victor Parry Cup, Bloxwich League Extra Trophy and Walsall Charity Cup. They scored 120 goals in 38 matches, winning 24, losing 6 and drawing 8. Players' list; N. Painter, H. Holloway, J. Wesley, R. Buckley, T. Ray, G. Dorsett, F. Sergeant, R. Wiggin, N. Hall, J. Parkes, J. Richards, S. Dukes, E. Painter, H. Benton, (sec.) H.J. Moseley (capt.), J. Ansell.

CANNOCK TOWN FOOTBALL CLUB taken from a cigarette card. The club was formed in 1868 and played in the Birmingham League. It was described as having a 'Fine reputation for providing keen football'. The club was wound up in 1937. Back, left to right: F. Harding, H. Cliff, T. Reary (trainer), J. Davis, J. Haddaway, R. Talbot, F. Allen, T. Jones. F.R.I. Galley, C. Raines, T. Galley, N. Rowe, E. Parkes (capt.) Seated: J. Wilding, G. Wilding.

HEATH HAYES UNITY CRICKET CLUB in 1909 at the Recreation Ground, Heath Hayes.

NORTON PRIMS FOOTBALL CLUB 1929. Based on the Primitive Methodist Church there is quite a spread of ages represented in this team.

DANDIES JAZZ BAND 1938. Jazz bands are another local feature with a long history. This band was based at Norton Canes.

AN OUTING TO BEAUDESERT HALL. Many of the colliery companies provided outings for miners' wives and families. This group from Chasetown are travelling on a specially cleaned coal wagon pulled by the Loco 'Griffin'. Beaudesert was the home of the Marquis of Anglesey and the final stage of the trip would have been made by wagonette.

A DRESS PARADE at Pye Green Methodist Chapel in around 1936.

MEN PLAYING PITCH AND FOB in Chasetown. This game was a form of marbles and wagers were made on the outcome.

REGULARS AT THE WHITE LION, Cheslyn Hay at the turn of the century. This group called themselves 'The Old Boys'. Mr Bill Williams is first on the left in the back row.

THE STAR AND GARTER BOWLING CLUB, Wedges Mills, in the 1920s. The photograph was taken on what is now part of the car park of The Winking Frog. Back row, from left to right: fourth left, Cornelius Pearson; Ern Barlow; Billy Haycock junior; George Eardley; Jack Smith; Cyril Haycock; Archie Haycock; Sam Belcher and Jim Dawson. Front, standing left, -?-. Seated, left to right: Joe Starkey; Charlie Pearce; Syd Belcher; Harold Belcher; Lionel Fairley, manager of the Hawkins Pit; Fred Dando who kept the Star and Garter; Billy Haycock senior; the man with the beard is Bernie Bill.

THE WOODMAN BOWLING CLUB, Cheslyn Hay, July 1961 when they won the Cheslyn Hay and District Butchers Bowling Cup. The man bowling is 'Knocker' Evans. Their skipper was 17 year old P. Spencer. The final was played on the ancient bowling green in the centre of Cannock. The groundsman at the time was J. Keddie.

THE CANAL MISSION, Old Hednesford Road. A children's treat is seen leaving the wharf. Canal missions were established for the benefit of families that lived and worked on the canals.

A DAY TRIP TO ALTON TOWERS in 1904 by Hednesford Wesleyan Church Choir.

CYCLING CLUB MEMBERS in Station Road, Hednesford, in around 1909.

HAWKINS COLLIERY MECHANICS AND CRAFTSMEN'S OUTING in the 1920s. Such outings were an annual feature at the pit for many years. The charabanc is believed to be one of the first there was in the district – note the solid tyres!

LANDYWOOD WESLEYAN CHOIR OUTING in the early 1930s.

A DAY TRIP TO RHYL. Blackfords residents were carried by 13 coaches on 14 August 1948. Such visits were often organized by Working Men's Clubs.

HUSSELBEE'S PIG STY in the 1920s. Many local people kept pigs in backyard sties. It was both a form of relaxation and a useful supplement to a household's income.

THE HUNT meets outside the Fleur de Lys Inn.

THE WINIFRED, a Pleasure Steamer that used to operate on Norton Pool. The boat was originally brought to the pool to carry slag from the Black Country used for reinforcing the dam. It was run as a pleasure craft by Mr Donaldson but was not a commercial success. It was eventually left to rot by the side of the pool.

LEISURE PURSUITS ON CANNOCK CHASE. Rowing boats could be hired on Pottal Pool in the 1930s. There is a quarry on this site now.

THE BATHING LIDO at Pottal Pool at around the same time.

THE SANDHOLE AT SHOAL HILL on Bank Holiday Monday 1933.

ACKNOWLEDGEMENTS

This book would not have been possible without access to the photographic collections of Cannock and Burntwood libraries, by kind permission of the Librarians, Lynne Stanley and Mary Pochin. The photographs we have selected were originally donated by many different people and organizations. We wish to acknowledge their generosity and also apologise if we have unwittingly missed anyone from the following list;

Mrs Bhagerutty • John Bradbury • The *Cannock Advertiser* • Godwin Mrs Jesse Gough • Mrs Hayward • Mrs Pat Hill • Arthur Hitchenson Mrs Hood • C.O. Hughes • Mr C. Ives • Mr Johnson • Mr and Mrs Jones Jukes • Mrs Kinber • Mrs Ethel Markall • Miss G.E.M. Moore • Mr J. Moore Mrs Moore • Morris • Mr A. Paine • Fred Parsons • Madge Perks Mr Pope • Mr O. Roadway • Mrs Robinson • Mrs E. Rogers • Mrs E. Smith Mr C. Stephens • Mr Tonks • Mrs Tooth • Mrs Tranter • Mr Turner Mrs E. Turvey • W. Waltho • E. Whitehouse • Walter Wright.

We also wish to thank the staffs of both libraries for their time and assistance, in particular Mr Don Brown and Miss Margaret Kingston of Cannock Library. Equally important were the individuals who loaned photographs from their personal collections or gave valuable advice and information. We wish to thank;

Mr Jack Belcher • Mr Kelvin Belcher • Mr David Brown • Mr John Bryant Mr and Mrs E. Clewley • Miss Kath Cross • Mr Trevor Groves Miss D.A. Holdcroft • Mr Roger Knowles • Miss Peg Malpass Mr Bill Matthews • Mr Derek Mills • Miss Elsie Shaw • Mr Percy Shaw Mr B. Stokes • Mr Eric Roberts • Mr and Mrs T. Thompson • Miss Wilson.

We would also like to thank Dudley Fowkes of Stafford Record Office for permission to reproduce part of the Rules of Hednesford Training Ground from the Anglesey papers Ref. D603/K/27/13.